CLEARING THE MASK

poems by

Gay Parks Rainville

Finishing Line Press
Georgetown, Kentucky

CLEARING THE MASK

For Mark

Copyright © 2021 by Gay Parks Rainville
ISBN 978-1-64662-413-3 First Edition
All rights reserved under International and Pan-American Copyright Conventions. No part of this book may be reproduced in any manner whatsoever without written permission from the publisher, except in the case of brief quotations embodied in critical articles and reviews.

ACKNOWLEDGMENTS

I would like to extend my heartfelt gratitude to the remarkable poets who have mentored and enriched my development as a poet: from Warren Wilson—Rodney Jones, Christine Kitano, Maurice Manning, Heather McHugh, Chase Twichell, and Alan Williamson; from the Kenyon Review Writers Workshop—David Baker, the late Stanley Plumly, and Mary Szybist; from my favorite online classes—Chanda Feldman and Will Schutt; and from Denison University—the late Paul Bennett.

I also am grateful for the steadfast encouragement and inspiration I received over the years from my beloved friends and family, particularly my Uncle Stanley Barlow, who published his first collection of poems, *Swimming Laps in August*, at the age of 76, and my husband Mark, who is my first and most treasured reader.

Publisher: Leah Huete de Maines
Editor: Christen Kincaid
Cover Art: Heidi Rainville
Author Photo: Mark D. Rainville
Cover Design: Elizabeth Maines McCleavy

Order online: www.finishinglinepress.com
also available on amazon.com

Author inquiries and mail orders:
Finishing Line Press
PO Box 1626
Georgetown, Kentucky 40324
USA

Table of Contents

I.

Driving in Snow Through the Blue Ridge Mountains,
I Hear a Radio Alert that North Korean Nuclear Missiles
are Headed for Hawaii 1
Emerald Coast Ghazal 2
Sitting Up With My Husband 3
Horseshoe Crab Tankas 4
Site Fidelity 5
Coastal Dune Lake 6
Buying Miami Beach 7

II.

Cancer Valley 8
Seventy-One 9
Roller Skating With My Mother, 1969 10
My Father's Pulpit Robe 12
Bay Bridge Tankas 13

III.

Cracking His Chest 14
Perfect Strangers 16
To My Nephew, the Marathoner,
Three Years after His Brother Die 17
Clockwork 18
Returning to 11 Kent Place 19
Trees, Grass, Sky 20

IV.

Quitting Time 21
Eagles Fans Ascending...22
For S. P..23
Reenactment 25
Spider Web Haiku...26
Red Bird Tankas..27
Neighbor Girls 28

V.

Coloring..29
Waiting for the Great Valley Flyer 30
Ready or Not 31
Cohabitation..32
Sternum to the Sky 33
Meditation on White Hair..34
Ode to a Sunken Farm Village...35

I.

Driving in Snow Through the Blue Ridge Mountains, I Hear a Radio Alert that North Korean Nuclear Missiles are Headed for Hawaii

With black ice forming and snow swirling in fits
   I drive alone on Interstate 26, threading a mountain range
      wrapped in a blue haze now turning silver,
         gauze draping the hills' bare trees,
            a gray on gray mesh stenciled against the steel sky.

My breath stops and starts in tempo with the wipers'
   futile *sque-thump*, *sque-thump*, and my heart begins to tighten
      as it did when I was five, careening around these same mountains
         through a December ice storm, my father at the wheel,
            his family packed tight to see his mother one last time,
               my face pressed into the sofa cushion
                  he placed on the backseat floor
                     between my two older siblings' feet.

As ice thickens and the horizon disappears, I dwell on the panic felt
   by people in Hawaii before they learned that the nuclear missile alert
      was a false alarm, the terrified father kneeling at the edge
         of a manhole, helping his children crawl into the sewer
            one at a time before texting his parents goodbye.

From across the miles I can hear my dog howling
   at shooting stars, at sirens blaring,
      and I feel my body struggling to breathe beneath the waves
         as it did when I nearly drowned while diving
            deep in the Caribbean, surrendering again to the desire
               to escape, to ascend from the depths of the sea,
                  my regulator dropping to the sandy bottom
                     salt water flooding my mask.

Emerald Coast Ghazal

The lighthouse burns through fog beyond the shore of the gulf.
Its siren mouths our names into the roar of the gulf.

A flying billboard wraps the sky *Will you marry me?*
We kick and swat and sweat until we bore of the gulf.

Children tunnel the beach for sea stars beneath tarballs.
Petrol spills rainbows into open sores of the gulf.

Shiny carcasses of laughing gulls pockmark the strand
while a dirty blizzard blankets the floor of the gulf.

Your parents' caskets lie above the sea here, *Gay*, so
why do you float inchoate in the lore of the gulf?

Sitting Up With My Husband

I dream about my father dying
again, his sea blue eyes wide
and mute before me as I count
his breaths from a hollowed mouth
I do not recognize.

Beside me you drift against sleep
playing solitaire on your iPad,
hoping for a dreamless night,
to be spared visions of your parents
pleading with you to move in,
to let them drive.

Lie down, my love. Close your eyes
and dive with me. Let's descend
together past—not past but through—
the muck of sorrow and regret, and float
among our loved and unloved ones,
measuring our breaths against each other's,
slow and deep.

Horseshoe Crab Tankas

They suggested death—
war helmets lining the beach,
menacing ruins
of huge nine-eyed arthropods
marring the crystal white sand.

But death was not there,
just remains of old armor
outgrown by fossils
still living, still swimming deep
in larger shells, upside down.

Site Fidelity

My friend returns to Holgate every June
and every morning walks the streets
of his summer bayside neighborhood,
inspecting gravel driveways and yards
for signs of camouflage—patches of sand
the mother terrapins use to cover
their buried clutches of pale-pink eggs
before returning home to brackish marshes.

Racing against the appetites of raccoons
and crows and mink, he excavates the nests he finds
and carries the eggs in a frayed beach towel
to the safe harbor of his neighbor's backyard hatchery
where they incubate in leathery shells.

In August, he hydrates the hatchlings in his garage
in plastic kiddie pools filled with fresh water,
then releases them to their coastal marshland.
He hopes they will restore the cordgrass,
feeding on its predators—periwinkle snails,
ribbed mussels, fiddler crabs.

Coastal Dune Lake

The elevated trail takes us there, past oak scrub,
swamp titi, southern magnolias, across

thickets of lupine and spoon flowers. We weave through
golden aster, pitcher plants and cattails until

we reach the quartz sand dunes undulating under
a patchwork of sea oats. We climb to the top, where

we stop, breathless, above the black pool flickering
between the knolls. Lilly pads sway against sand grass.

Beyond the berm, laughing gulls and snowy plovers
wade in the outfall that spills into the Gulf.

Buying Miami Beach

Be bold. It's a buyer's market after all.
You can bid on a foreclosed rancher
where reef squid and octopuses
moved into the garage after the last king tide.
You'd have to gut it, of course,
and raise it level with the trees.

Or I can sell you a prefab McMansion
on stilts, floating twenty feet into the air.
You can choose a Victorian
or a craftsman model. Each comes wrapped
in a porch where you can rock away
your afternoons, sipping martinis,
watching the sun set,
listening to the waves slap
against the concrete pilings beneath you
while the sea rises above the streets
and Miami Beach disappears.

It'll feel like Stiltsville,
where 80-year old shacks
now slump on long skinny legs
above the sand flats of Biscayne Bay.
So don't worry about buying beachfront.
You'll soon be living on the water
no matter what.

II.

Cancer Valley

Before *Mother Jones*
renamed it in '78, I ran
through the valley almost every day

along one-lane roads
that snaked down the hill—
from Summit to Edgewood—

across the flat streets of downtown
to the Kanawha River,

through benzene-clogged air
trapped by the hill chain,

then reversed course
back up to our home,

where I could look down
through our picture window and see
the valley's green lushness
and gold capitol dome,

but the smog blocked my view of the sites
located further down the river—

DuPont, Monsanto, Union Carbide, FMC,
Allied Chemical, Diamond Shamrock—

the toxin makers that killed my mother
and her best friend Helen.

Seventy-One

Your age, my Sun Belt sister,
when you first spotted them—
two melanomas, one on each cheek,
slowly inked by the sun while you squinted
away your suburban mom years
tending to your daughters' lives
in backyard pools, softball fields,
and open-air malls.

Our mother's age, too, when she died,
her own body finally destroying
her liver altogether, decades after she breathed
Kanawha Valley's opaque, bile-green air—
bitter fumes we tasted whenever we entered
the sunless outdoors; long before I knew
the meaning of carcinogen, autoimmune,
primary biliary cirrhosis; long before I understood
the full bounty of the Fortune 500 companies
that took over our river banks, the toxic byproducts
of their success—vinyl chlorine, benzene, dioxin,
methyl isocyanate . . . .

This, the environment's revenge, battering
our DNA into mutation. After your surgery,
the twin oval scars affix to your new face
like sealing wax stamps.

While your face that I know
starts to disappear,
I try not to look away
as I did when our redheaded mother
began to turn yellow, when every tissue
changed color—even her freckles,
the whites of her eyes.

Roller Skating With My Mother, 1969

Before roller disco
   and strobe lights
made skating at the rink
   with one's mother
uncool,
   before I became good enough
to skate with teenage boys,

before my mother stopped showing up
   in her powder-blue culottes
and matching vest to fetch me
   home from junior high,
the outfit my friends snickered
   about behind my back,

before she lost 20 pounds
   on that liquid diet,
and everybody said she looked
   like Nancy Reagan,

before my father convinced her
   he wasn't having an affair
with the church secretary Elaine
   who made him polyester neckties
and pocket squares—

   I agree to roller skate
with my mother in public.

At first I stumble
   and palm the wall
as we skate together
   along the outside lane,
her arm around my waist.

Then she releases me
 and floats to the center of the rink
where she skates alone
 forwards and backwards, her turns
and crossovers quick and smooth,
 and I see a flash of the girl
I'd studied in old black-and-whites—
 my mother as a teenager
wearing a swing skirt and tap shoes,
 dancing solo in the middle
of a school gymnasium,
 her arms stretched out to her sides,
hands flexed up, her left knee bent
 and lifted behind the right,
a crowd of other teenagers
 sitting on the bleachers
hands raised in the air.

My Father's Pulpit Robe

I discovered it again
when we tracked down my father,
lost and collapsed on a sidewalk
in downtown Jasper from trying
to catch up with his second wife
who fled back to her Indiana home
after watching him Sunday
after Sunday, standing in the pulpit
of the tiny Laurel Hill church,
staring out at the half-empty pews
unable to say a word.

It was in the trunk of his stranded '97 Lincoln
among two torn madras suitcases, AAA
TripTik maps of every state between Florida
and Indiana, a half-empty box of bran flakes,
a bunch of blackened bananas. I found it inside
the frayed garment bag that was draped
over a pile of rubber-banded yellowed pages,
his ten-year-old sermons, written in longhand,
double-sided, very few words crossed out.

When I unzipped the bag, the black robe smelled
as I had remembered, his perspiration
from wearing it over dress shirts and suit pants
on Augusta's hot, humid Sunday mornings,
the white silk stole someone from a women's
circle made for him, now grey and stained.

The sleeves, the bell-shaped sleeves
with their velvet stripes were exactly
the same as when I, as a first grader,
used to tug on the left sleeve and beg
him to make a muscle so I could hang
on his bicep while he stood at the church
entrance, his right sleeve extended out
to his parishioners as he leaned down
to shake their hands, squeeze their shoulders.

Bay Bridge Tankas

I knead his old hand
massaging each cold finger
as his breathing stops
then starts for a few seconds
and he catches life again.

He can still hear me
so I talk about the cop
who escorted him
across the Chesapeake Bay
when panic seized his body.

That night in the fog
the crest of the thin Bay Bridge
eighteen stories high
disappeared altogether
paralyzing my father.

He begins to choke
and then his shoulders shudder
as he gasps for air
resisting his next journey
to an invisible place.

So I promise him
if he will loosen his grip
I will take over
and drive him up and across
the opaque and stormy Bay.

III.

Cracking His Chest

The surgeon splits
my brother's sternum in two

to get at the heart of his locked body,
to make it pulse again

with three new tributaries
from his boney legs

bypassing the blockage—
an accumulation

of our father's family history
of hardened arteries and brittle tempers,

of my brother's own love
for Camel Wides.

The doctor cuts through his long torso
stretched taut from buried images—

    the steak knife he once thrust toward my face
    and threatened to kill me with
    when he was sixteen, slouched
    in front of a Saran-wrapped supper
    the rest of us had finished over an hour earlier,
    and I was nine, sitting upright beside him
    whining that he was making us late
    for prayer meeting again;

the flash of my father, the minister,
lunging at the knife, wrestling him
to the ground, blue-lined pages
of bible-study notes floating
onto the kitchen floor;

then, years later, the permanent scowl
of his unhappy wife, now demented,
and the body of his troubled son, slumped over
dead from an accidental drug overdose.

My brother texts me not to worry,
that his metal breastplate is fireproof,

better than the original
for protecting the heart,

and attaches a selfie of the zipper scar
on his now deflated chest.

Perfect Strangers

Married over 40 years, they still share a bed.
She awakes each morning to him
embracing her. He seems like a loving man,
who tries to anchor her to this world,
but she does not know him. He is to her
a perfect stranger.

She sinks in sleep to memories kept alive
in dreams. A boy (*her son David?*) sits
beside her in the family room of their house
on Mineola Lane. He is fourteen again, living
again, guffawing with her at fuzzy images
on the old Zenith.

The man is gently shaking her now, saying
Love, get up; it's almost time for day care.
He resembles a man in a picture on the wall—
a younger man smiling next to three other people
she does not know, two tall boys and a woman
standing arm-in-arm between them.

To My Nephew, The Marathoner, Three Years After His Brother Died

If only you were

from the starting block

your own lane

of your parents' lives

you could clear

the debris

left behind

instead of enduring.

a sprinter

who could race

avoiding the long haul

a hurdler

at top speed

your brother

when he overdosed

Clockwork

No, it's not clockwork
anymore. You don't say
wave to Mom when we
drive away. I don't look
back as the house recedes
or search the bay window
for her silhouette
for her open palm to rise
and turn, once, twice.
She did not know
it was time for us to leave
or that we had arrived.

Returning to 11 Kent Place

We make the sharp turn into the cul-de-sac
and see only giant knolls of rubble
where your parents' home once stood—
the sole remains of the mid-century
your father designed and refused to outlive.

If I squint hard enough I can still make out
the tree-canopied backyard where he mounted bird feeders
every May hoping for cardinals and every June
spent his weekends trapping squirrels from the feeders
in shoebox-sized cages and releasing them
into the wooded park down the street.

Smelling the familiar scent of the neighbor's raked leaves,
I shut my eyes so I can look into the family room bay window
and see the backs of your parents sitting on the sofa,
shoulders touching. I cup my ear with the palm of my hand
to hear your mother's voice, soft and fretful (*where are we?*)
and your father's hoarse whispers (*we are home my love*).

Trees, Grass, Sky

They're all she can talk about now
that they've surfaced. I recoil

as they spill from her, mucus-filled
horrors from her childhood, released

by her new therapist—a brick
floor first, cold to bare feet, then trees,

running through trees, grass, her back
against grass, black sky, so black,

wrapping around her, holding her
down. Unable to feel the squeeze

of her husband's hand
or hear my sobbing,

she sees only silver-haired thighs
above her and the sky, the black sky.

IV.

Quitting Time

What thoughts I have of you, Dennis O'Driscoll,
my office poet, as I make the thirty-floor
descent from this place I call work.

I wonder, do you miss it? Your work, I mean,
now that you're dead. After all, you said having a job
provides endless insights into ordinary life. But it wasn't

life you wrote about, my worker poet. Your poems breathed
death—*ordinary* death, perhaps, but death just the same.
After all, only the death-obsessed could write the lines:

Someone is dressing up for death today, a change of skirt or tie
eating a final feast of buttered sliced pan, tea
scarcely having noticed the erection that was his last

I could have used your help today, my death poet. See,
Franny, the red-headed secretary who sits outside my office,
died this morning. But she wasn't one of your *someones*.

No, Franny *knew* she was dying. Kept a stockpile of wigs—
all red, just for us. Filled the candy jar before she left
so we wouldn't notice that she is no longer here.

Eagles Fans Ascending

The roar begins underground
as we spiral up the subway stairs
to join the five-mile mob
shouting *E-A-G-L-E-S*
from South Philly to the Art Museum,
devoted worshippers of a team
that let us down Sunday
after Sunday, season after season,
for fifty-one years, a swarm
of emerald arms flapping
at victorious players who float by,
waving their cigars and kissing
their long-idolized Lombardi trophy.

A drone flying overhead captures
the moment when a multitude
of bowed heads in jewel-toned caps
and parka hoods—looped like rows
of rosary beads around Eakins Oval—
pauses to remember friends and family
who did not live to see this day. Some fans
clutch deceased loved ones in brass urns
while a man in a Jerome Brown jersey
strides among the convocation
sprinkling the dust of his grandfather
from a white envelope.

For S.P.

From across the fourth-floor dorm room
   we share, I envy the back
of your ballerina body hunched
   over the desk, cramming for finals,
your wild, wiry hair knotted in a twist
   above your Balanchine neck,
your right hand hovering
   above the dining-hall plate
piled high with cigarette butts,
   the signed black and white
of Margot Fonteyn barely visible
   behind a teetering stack
of coffee-stained mugs.

Earlier that semester,
   during our spring break trip
to Chicago, you lit up
   a joint at B.L.U.E.S.,
heckled the band, and hit
   on the lead singer.
The crowd laughed—
   it was the 70s after all—
but when you returned to the hotel
   the next morning, your peasant blouse
ripped at the shoulder, I knew
   not to ask what happened.

Back on campus now
   for our 40th reunion, I climb
to our old room and stare
   at the familiar door, locked
for the summer. During our class
   cocktail party, someone asks me
what happened to you—if you
   ever became a public defender
as you had planned. I tell them the truth,
   that the last time I saw you
was in '83 when you and your Toledo
   boyfriend showed up at my apartment door
in Chicago, stoned out of your minds,
   looking for a place to crash.
How I turned you away.

Tonight, when I Google your name
   searching for answers, headlines
from the *Toledo Blade* fill the screen:
Toledo trio convicted at trial
of forging will to steal $2.2 million.
Former Toledo attorney sentenced
to nine years in fraud case. Then, a mug shot
   of a woman I still recognize flashes
on my laptop: a much older, dissipated,
   scary version of you—your high cheekbones
flattened into a square face, your bright
   hazel eyes now vacant slits
inside heavy folds of skin
   beneath angular, penciled-in arches
where your thick oval brows once grew,
   the ironic tilt of your smile collapsed
into a horizontal line.

Reenactment

Like the townspeople
who every year reenact
the Paoli Massacre
where the British waged
and won a surprise attack,
I find myself in Malvern
again wandering the streets
of the tiny borough where I once lived
an anonymous life. I stroll down
Monument where every weekend
I once walked the dogs. Past the town
hoarder now stuffing a Wegman's tote bag
full of empty take-out boxes
from her neighbor's garbage can.
Past the house of the tombstone
salesman—his front yard lined
with sample headstones, displayed
for years. Past the middle-aged man
with the bell-topped Santa cap,
who stands by the payphone
outside the Wawa, announcing last night's
Sixers' score, his roommate clutching
to his ear a small transistor radio.

Spider Web Haiku

Three bayberry leaves
float in lace like marooned stars
their fall stopped midair

Silk threads ride a breeze
from spinneret to tree branch
tightropes span the lawn

An orb-weaver feasts
on a broken gossamer
recycling the silk

Laden with debris
autumn's abandoned cobwebs
gild the burning bush

Red Bird Tankas

I flocked with others
to the Alabama town
of Alabaster
to see a yellow cardinal
perched on a backyard feeder.

Mustard not yellow,
opined the bird curator
when scrutinizing
the astonishing color
through binocular lenses.

Carotene deprived,
the expert hypothesized
from the frayed feathers.
Not enough sweet potatoes
to make this bird's plumage red.

Then I remembered
my tiny redheaded friend
who once ate carrots
and nothing else to maintain
her gaunt frame and coral hue.

Her long copper hair
grazed the hem of her dresses
and her orange arms flailed
when she chirped her staccato
opinions—high pitched, breathless.

Neighbor Girls

It's early spring and bare young trees rise
   from patches of black-dyed mulch that dot
     the green banks of the dry retention basin
        landscaped to look like a park.

From my window two stories up I can see them   running
   toward the edge of the ditch   five first-grade girls   their fists
     flying above their heads. One by one they plunge
       over the ridge   somersaulting to the bottom.

My window is closed so I hear no sound
   but I can see their mouths stretched wide with laughter
     with the thrill of hurtling down the hill
       no looking around or up
         to see who might be watching.

V.

Coloring

What to do with the red? Cover it with yellow to make the sun rise.

>Yes, let's get rid of the red, the whole deafening
>screech of it. It's orange I want to hear.
>Give it to me mottled. Let me see the streaks,
>the white page showing. I need to smell it, taste it,
>the full carotene of it.

If you mix the orange sky with the grass, both will turn brown.

>I need the brown. Don't mute or flatten it
>or add any white. Let me feel the rich grainy earth
>murk of it, breathe it, roll in it, live in it,
>be buried in it.

Once the sun rises, don't let it touch the blue sky.

>I want my suns green. Suns I can see
>without squinting.

Don't smear the black tree trunk against the white clouds.

>You should know by now.
>I live for gray.

Waiting for the Great Valley Flyer

Rain drums the roof. Windows rattle against wind gusts.
Tuesday's trash truck is here already, idling in the dark.

I can hear the thud of bins being dropped mid-street; one rolls
away toward the distant *clack clap* of the departing commuter train.

I listen through the frantic barking of the neighbor's dog
and the murder of crows cawing overhead

for the apnea gasp of my husband's next breath. I look forward
to boarding the express train and the *shhhh* of its quiet car,

and still lying there, think about my brother-in-law
sitting at his father's funeral with his hearing aids in his pocket.

Ready or Not

All three run past me
their great aunt as I hold open
the door to my new home
inviting them to lose themselves
inside the strange house, to enter
the cavernous U-Haul wardrobes,
the heavy folds of unhung living
room drapes, the hollow crevices
peering from beneath bedframes
and among the shadows of teetering
columns of books stacked crisscross
between heaps of dumped winter coats.

In the sudden stillness
I stand alone in the dark pantry
and listen for the muffled counting
to rise from the sofa pillows,
bracing myself for the familiar
full-throated scream.

Cohabitation

Now that my husband travels for work I sit
alone with the lights off most December nights
since the floor-to-ceiling blinds for our new house
have not yet arrived and our windows look out
onto the backyards of strangers who huddle
around fire pits until midnight drinking beer
and shouting to one another against the constant caw
of crows roosting in the bare oak tree that towers
over the neighborhood. Tonight, I grope the still
empty home from kitchen to bathroom to bedroom
and lie awake contemplating the solitude of the fox
curled in the snowbank of the nearby ravine, wrapped
in its red tail, and the groundhog that will sleep all
winter long alone in its deep windowless burrow
beneath our screened-in porch hidden until spring
from its predators. I await the nightly flash
of the motion detector light above the patio door
triggered by our neighbor's wandering dog.

Sternum to the Sky!

My cousin Ann interjects
        when I complain about my sloping
back, my budding
        dowager's hump,
my fear of falling—
        a mantra
her personal trainer half her age
        sings to her
whenever her trunk begins to tilt
        toward the treadmill.

This right-angle shape my body
        wants to make—the ground's tug
on my chest unrelenting—
        like my father-in-law in the last
year of his life after he ran out of reasons
        to look up or forward
and spent his days shuffling from room to room,
        torso parallel to the floor, feeding
and bathing and dressing his wife
        who no longer knew his name.

Yes, Ann, let's chant *sternum to the sky!*
        as we age and try to defy
gravity's pull on our limbs.
        No more watching our steps
or clutching the handrails.
        No more slouching to the corners
or saying sorry for our slower gait.
        Or is it too late for us to rise up
from the shadows of our younger selves
        to gaze again at the sun,
to climb the stairs two at a time,
        to revel again in the thrill of falling
head over heels, our clenched hearts
        opening, saluting the moon?

Meditation on White Hair

If, when we get old, we dye
our white hair back to brown,

do we become like the weasel
in summer when its fur matches

the landscape—drab, muted, invisible?
If we keep our hair white, will it

stun the eye, will it turn younger heads
in our direction—like the sleek winter coat

of a stoat, prized by the luxury fur trade
and worn by royalty and Marilyn Monroe;

like the enormous snowy owls that migrate
to Philadelphia's airfields each winter,

drawing birders to gaze upon their ghostly wings
soaring just beneath mortal planes?

Ode to a Sunken Farm Village
      Marsh Creek Lake, Pennsylvania

We are your celestial bodies,
gliding across the night sky
in kayaks and canoes,
past ducks and grebes
and coots, above the stars
the state has stocked.
They, too, have names:
bass, walleye, trout.

Today our blended family
crowds your gray heavens.
Motley planets, we drift
toward my granddaughter
who floats with her parents
in a row boat celebrating
birthday number two.

I told her about you.
She wants to know
if she can come visit you
some day, down there,
to touch the ghosts
of your chimneys,
feel the steeples
of your churches.

Gay Parks Rainville is a poet and an attorney, as well as a former high school English teacher and modern dancer. She graduated from The MFA Program for Writers at Warren Wilson College in 2019. This is her debut chapbook collection of poetry.

The daughter of a left-leaning, literature-loving Presbyterian minister and a deeply religious, reliably witty bible teacher/homemaker, Rainville grew up in North Carolina, Georgia, and West Virginia during a time when young women were discouraged from seeking careers outside of the home. Perhaps because her broad-minded parents raised her to believe that she could do anything she set her mind to, she set her mind to doing lots of things before finally exploring her love for poetry writing. After graduating from Denison University in 1977, she moved to Chicago where she obtained an M.A.T. degree from Northwestern University's School of Education and Social Policy; studied, taught, and performed modern dance; taught high school English; and, in 1985-1988, attended Northwestern's Pritzker School of Law. Since 1988, she has practiced law in Philadelphia as a commercial litigator.

Although Rainville studied poetry composition during her senior year of college and had a poem published in the college literary magazine, *Exile*, she did not begin writing poems in earnest until 2011. Before entering Warren Wilson's MFA program six years later, she focused on developing her poetry-writing craft by attending several sessions of the *Kenyon Review*'s intense weeklong Writers Workshop and participating in various in-person and online classes.

An avid rambler, Rainville receives much of her inspiration for poems while taking long walks throughout the two towns where she and her husband currently divide their time, Media, Pennsylvania and Destin, Florida.

www.ingramcontent.com/pod-product-compliance
Lightning Source LLC
LaVergne TN
LVHW041552070426
835507LV00011B/1058